DUTCH OVEN
COOKING

BEFORE YOU BEGIN...

To cook outdoors in a Dutch oven, let a wood fire burn down until you get white hot coals and then break them into chunks about the size of charcoal briquettes, or simply preheat charcoal briquettes in a chimney starter. Count these hot coals and arrange them under the pot and on the lid as directed in the recipes.

The cooking times in this book are estimates because actual time depends on the weather and how hot your coals are. Start with the number of coals listed, but check your food periodically and then adjust the heat up or down as needed.

To cook at 325° - 350°, here's a general formula:

Dutch oven's diameter *(in inches)* X 2 = hot coals needed

Add 2 coals to increase the temperature about 25°. Remove 2 coals to decrease the temperature about 25°. After some practice, you can estimate the heat without counting coals.

Printed in the United States of America
by G&R Publishing Co.

Distributed By:

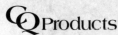

507 Industrial Street
Waverly, IA 50677

ISBN-13: 978-1-56383-510-0
Item #2912

THE CAMP-STYLE DUTCH OVEN

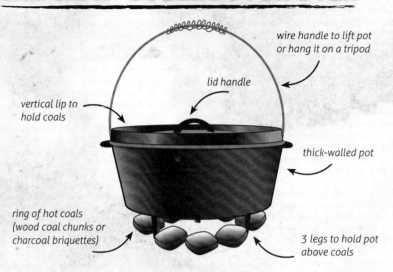

wire handle to lift pot
or hang it on a tripod

lid handle

vertical lip to
hold coals

thick-walled pot

ring of hot coals
(wood coal chunks or
charcoal briquettes)

3 legs to hold pot
above coals

What size to buy? The **10" (4-quart)** and **12" (6-quart)** Dutch ovens are very versatile. To serve a crowd, consider a **deep 12" (8-quart)** one. *(Don't over-fill with food; leave at least 1" at the top.)*

Season it well: Coat all surfaces of the pot and lid with a thin layer of vegetable oil or shortening and set them upside down on the upper rack in a 350° oven to heat for 1 hour. *(Cover the bottom rack with foil to catch any drips.)* Turn off the oven and let cool completely. Do this periodically to prevent rust and maintain a smooth nonstick cooking surface.

Clean it right every time: Hand-wash the pot and lid in very hot water without soap. Use a plastic scraper, nylon scrubber, or stiff nylon brush to remove food; rinse well and wipe dry. Set over warm coals to evaporate any remaining moisture and then rub lightly with vegetable oil.

Store it until next time: Insert a small pad of paper towels between the lid and pot so air can circulate and store in a dry place. If rust appears, scrub it off with steel wool and reseason before using.

THESE TOOLS MAKE DUTCH OVEN COOKING A SNAP...

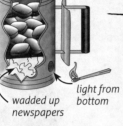

wadded up newspapers   *light from bottom*

Charcoal chimney starter: to light charcoal briquettes quickly without using lighter fluid

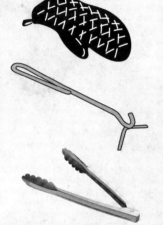

Heavy–duty cooking mitts: to protect hands when handling hot cookware

Lid lifter: to remove the heavy lid without dumping coals into the pot. Use it to rotate the lid during cooking, too – just hook it under the lid handle and turn.

Long tongs: to move hot coals safely

Metal garbage can lid: to provide a dry, firm cooking base if the fire pit is wet, soft, or uneven. *(Just dig a small hole for the handle and set the lid upside down before building your fire on it.)*

baking pan

metal nuts

Risers: to lift a baking pan off the bottom of the Dutch oven. Set metal nuts *(or an inverted metal pan)* in the pot and place a pan of food on the riser. To bake, cover the pot and put a ring of coals underneath with more coals on the lid.

LET THE COOKING BEGIN!

The temperature inside a Dutch oven depends on the number and placement of hot coals or the distance of the pot from the heat. Sometimes you spread the hot coals in a flat layer underneath the Dutch oven – **this gives plenty of heat for boiling, browning, or frying.**

But **to bake, simmer, or roast** foods, you'll need heat from both the bottom and top, so arrange some hot coals in a ring underneath the pot and place more coals on the lid.

gaps for legs

Rotate the pot and lid every 10 to 15
minutes to prevent hot spots. Just lift the pot off the coals by the wire handle and rotate the whole thing clockwise ⅓ turn – then set it back down on the heat. Rotate the lid ⅓ turn in the opposite direction *(counterclockwise).*

add more coals to lids

Check your food often to see how fast it's
cooking. Coals get very hot but they tend to burn out and lose heat after 30 to 45 minutes so if something needs to cook longer, you may need to add fresh hot coals to maintain the cooking temperature.

Stacked Cooking is efficient! Set one Dutch
oven on top of another so both foods cook with shared coals. Try cooking soup or stew in the bottom pot and bread or dessert on top.

Tripod Cooking is a good way to simmer
food. Hang a pot over hot coals on a tripod and relax as it cooks. Move the pot closer to the coals for more heat or raise it higher for less heat.

5

CIDER BEEF STEW

extra
cook time

serves 8–10

You'll Need

⅓ C. flour

1½ tsp. paprika

Salt and black pepper
  to taste

2 lbs. beef stew meat

3 T. vegetable oil

2 C. hot water

1 T. beef bouillon granules

1½ C. apple cider

¼ C. ketchup

1 tsp. minced garlic

2 C. chopped cabbage

4 parsnips, peeled and
  chopped

1 onion, diced

2 C. baby carrots

continued on next page

You'll Need *continued*

- 4 potatoes, peeled and cubed
- 2 C. frozen green beans
- 1 (8.75 oz.) can whole kernel corn, drained
- 2 T. Worcestershire sauce

Directions

Mix the flour, paprika, salt, and pepper in a large zippered bag. Add meat cubes; seal bag and shake well to coat.

Spread about 24 hot coals in a flat layer under a **12" Dutch oven**. Heat oil and brown the meat on all sides. Stir in water, bouillon, cider, ketchup, and garlic. Cover pot with lid.

Rearrange 12 of the hot coals in a ring under the Dutch oven and move remaining coals to the lid. Simmer until meat is tender, about 2 hours. Rotate pot and lid several times every hour and replenish coals as needed for simmering.

Add cabbage, parsnips, onion, carrots, potatoes, green beans, corn, and Worcestershire sauce. Cover and simmer with coals on top and bottom until vegetables are tender, about 1 hour. Rotate pot and replenish coals when necessary.

CINNAMON ROLLS

extra prep time

serves 12

You'll Need

24 frozen unbaked dinner rolls

1 C. brown sugar

5 tsp. ground cinnamon

½ C. chopped pecans

½ C. butter, melted

½ (16 oz.) can ready-to-use cream cheese frosting

Directions

Line a **12" Dutch oven** with foil and grease generously. Arrange the balls of frozen dough in the lined pot. Sprinkle with brown sugar, cinnamon, and pecans. Drizzle evenly with butter. Cover pot with lid and set aside until rolls are doubled in size, 3 to 5 hours.

To bake, set the Dutch oven on a ring of 8 hot coals and place about 15 coals on the lid. Bake 25 to 35 minutes or until golden brown and cooked through. Rotate the pot and lid twice during cooking and check doneness. Move some coals from the bottom ring to the center of lid during the last 5 to 10 minutes of cooking to promote browning. Lift foil to remove rolls from Dutch oven; frost rolls or pull apart and serve with a side of frosting for dipping.

Prep these cinnamon rolls and then let them rise in the pot while you're out having fun. Bake them later for ooey gooey goodness – never easier, never tastier!

GARLIC POTATO WEDGES

You'll Need

4 large Russet potatoes

½ C. butter

3 T. grated Parmesan cheese

½ tsp. garlic powder

1 tsp. seasoned salt

Dried parsley flakes

Directions

Wash the potatoes and cut each into 8 wedges. Set a **12" Dutch oven** over a few hot coals and melt the butter. Remove the pot from heat and coat potato wedges in butter; arrange them in a single layer in the pot.

In a small bowl, mix cheese, garlic powder, and seasoned salt; sprinkle over the potatoes. Top with some parsley flakes and cover pot with lid.

Set the Dutch oven on a ring of 9 hot coals and place about 16 coals on the lid. Cook about 30 minutes or until potatoes are fork-tender. Rotate pot and lid twice during cooking time and replenish coals on top as needed for even cooking.

These buttery potatoes make the perfect side dish for any meal. Mmmm...

Choose baking apples that will soften nicely when cooked. We used Jonagolds for pure deliciousness.

APPLE CRISP

fresh
& easy

serves 8–10

You'll Need

8 C. peeled, thinly sliced apples (about 5 large)

¾ C. sugar, divided

Juice from 1 lemon

Ground cinnamon to taste

¾ C. butter, divided

½ C. flour

¼ C. brown sugar

¼ tsp. salt

1 C. granola cereal

Directions

Line a **10" Dutch oven** with foil and grease lightly. Dump the apples into the lined pot and add ½ cup sugar, lemon juice, and a few shakes of cinnamon. Stir gently to combine. Cut ¼ cup butter into pieces and arrange evenly over the apples.

In a medium bowl, stir together remaining ¼ cup sugar, flour, brown sugar, salt, granola, and more cinnamon. Sprinkle flour mixture over apples and top evenly with pieces of the remaining ½ cup butter. Cover pot with lid.

Set the Dutch oven on a ring of 8 hot coals and place about 10 coals on the lid. Bake 25 to 35 minutes or until apples are tender and topping is lightly browned. Let coals burn down and rotate pot and lid every 8 to 10 minutes for even cooking. Move a few coals to the center of lid during the last few minutes of cooking to promote browning.

After your campfire burns down, cook this apple crisp for a perfectly sweet ending to the day.

13

GRANDMA'S MEATLOAF

extra
cook time

serves 10–12

You'll Need

2 lbs. ground beef

1 lb. ground sausage

2 eggs

1 C. chopped onion

1 celery rib, chopped

½ C. bread crumbs

4 bacon strips

Directions

Line a **10" Dutch oven** with foil. Combine the beef, sausage, eggs, onion, celery, and bread crumbs in a large bowl and mix well with hands until combined. Form the mixture into a square loaf inside the lined pot. Lay bacon over loaf and cover pot with lid.

Set the Dutch oven on a ring of 8 hot coals and place about 14 coals on the lid. Cook 1¼ to 1½ hours or until meat is cooked through *(internal temperature should be 160°)*. Rotate pot and lid every 15 minutes and replenish coals as needed to maintain heat. After 1 hour of cooking, add a few hot coals to the center of lid to brown the bacon. Drain off grease before serving.

Cook once, eat twice – just slice up any leftovers to have meatloaf sandwiches the next day.

CHICKEN TORTILLA SOUP

You'll Need

- 2 T. vegetable oil
- 1 onion, diced
- 1 tsp. minced garlic
- 1 (26 oz.) carton chicken stock
- 1 (28 oz.) can crushed tomatoes with juice
- 1 (4 oz.) can green chiles
- 2 tsp. chili powder
- 1 tsp. ground cumin
- 1 tsp. dried oregano
- 2 C. cooked, shredded chicken breast
- 1½ C. cooked elbow pasta
- 1 (8.5 oz.) can whole kernel corn, drained
- ¼ C. chopped fresh cilantro
- 1 lime, juiced
- Salt, black pepper, and cayenne pepper to taste

Directions

Spread about 24 hot coals in a flat layer under a **12" Dutch oven**. Heat the oil and add onion and garlic; cook until translucent, 2 to 3 minutes.

Stir in stock, tomatoes, chiles, chili powder, cumin, and oregano; bring to a simmer, pushing some of the hot coals to the side if soup cooks too fast. Cover pot with lid.

Rearrange half the hot coals in a ring under the Dutch oven and move remaining coals to lid. Let soup simmer 15 minutes, reducing the heat as needed for simmering.

Stir in chicken, pasta, corn, cilantro, lime juice, salt, pepper, and cayenne. Cover and cook until hot, about 10 minutes. Serve with sour cream, tortilla chips, sliced avocado, shredded cheese, and/or green onions.

You don't have to roll out these tender biscuits — just shape them with your hands and put them in the pot to cook.

CAMPSITE BISCUITS

serves 9

You'll Need

2½ C. self-rising flour, divided

½ to ¾ tsp. salt

1½ T. sugar

2 T. shortening

2 T. butter, softened

1¼ C. buttermilk

1½ T. butter, melted

Directions

Lightly oil a **10" Dutch oven**. In a bowl, combine 2 cups flour, salt, and sugar. Cut in shortening and soft butter until pea-size crumbs form. Stir in buttermilk until incorporated, but don't over-mix *(dough will be very wet)*. Let dough rest 2 to 3 minutes.

Place remaining ½ cup flour in a bowl and grease a large spoon. For each biscuit, drop a spoonful of dough into the flour. With floured hands, shape dough into a soft ball, shaking off excess flour. Set in oiled pot. Repeat to make a single layer of biscuits. Drizzle with melted butter and cover pot with lid.

Set the Dutch oven on a ring of 7 hot coals and place about 19 coals on the lid. Bake 20 to 30 minutes, rotating pot and lid twice during cooking. Move several coals to the center of lid near the end of cooking time to promote browning.

Short on time? Try baking refrigerated biscuit dough in a greased 8" round metal baking pan set on a riser inside the Dutch oven. Ready in 10 to 20 minutes!

HAWAIIAN KIELBASA

easy meal

serves 6

You'll Need

2 T. butter

1¼ C. water

1 (14 oz.) pkg. kielbasa sausage, sliced

1 red bell pepper, coarsely chopped

1 green bell pepper, coarsely chopped

1 (8 oz.) can pineapple chunks

1 (6.2 oz.) pkg. fast-cook long grain and wild rice mix with seasoning packet

½ C. pineapple preserves

Directions

Spread about 24 hot coals in a flat layer under a **12" Dutch oven**. Combine butter and water in the pot and bring to a boil.

Add the sausage, bell peppers, pineapple, rice, seasoning from packet, and pineapple preserves. Stir well and cover pot with lid.

Rearrange 10 of the hot coals in a ring under the Dutch oven and move the remaining coals to the lid. Cook 40 to 45 minutes, rotating pot and lid every 15 minutes and stirring twice; let coals burn down before replenishing. Remove from heat and let rest for 10 minutes before serving.

This delicious dish comes together in just a few minutes and cooks in less than an hour – Dutch oven paradise!

BREAKFAST BURRITOS

You'll Need

- ¾ lb. ground pork breakfast sausage
- 1 C. diced onion
- 1 C. diced green bell pepper
- 10 eggs
- 2 tsp. garlic powder
- 1 T. chili powder
- Salt and black pepper to taste
- 1 (4 oz.) can diced green chiles
- 10 (8") flour tortillas
- 1½ C. shredded Mexican 4-cheese blend
- Fire roasted tomato salsa

Directions

Spread about 21 hot coals in a flat layer under a **10" Dutch oven**. Cook the sausage, onion, and bell pepper until meat is brown and crumbly and vegetables are tender. Transfer the mixture to a large bowl; cover and keep warm.

In another bowl, whisk together eggs, garlic powder, chili powder, salt, pepper, and chiles. Push half the hot coals to one side and set the pot on remaining coals. Pour egg mixture into pot and scramble until cooked. Remove from heat and add scrambled eggs to sausage mixture; stir well. Wipe out the pot and line it with foil.

Scoop ⅓ to ½ cup egg and meat mixture onto each tortilla and sprinkle with cheese; roll up burrito-style, folding ends to enclose filling. Layer burritos in the pot and cover with lid. Set Dutch oven on a ring of 7 hot coals and place remaining coals on the lid, replenishing as needed to maintain heat. Bake 10 to 20 minutes or until cheese melts. Serve with salsa.

COWBOY BAKED BEANS

serves 12

You'll Need

½ lb. bacon, cut into 1" pieces

1½ lbs. ground beef

1 onion, diced

1 (15.5 oz.) can kidney beans, drained

1 (16 oz.) can pinto beans, drained

1 (15.5 oz.) can navy beans, drained

2 (15 oz.) cans pork and beans

1 C. barbecue sauce

¼ C. brown sugar

1 tsp. Worcestershire sauce

1 (1 oz.) pouch dry onion soup mix

Salt and black pepper to taste

Directions

Set a **12" Dutch oven** on a spread of hot coals. Fry the bacon until almost crisp. Carefully drain off the excess grease.

Return pot to heat and add beef and onion; cook until beef is brown and crumbly and onion is tender. Add all the beans plus the barbecue sauce, brown sugar, Worcestershire sauce, soup mix, salt, and pepper; stir well. Cook uncovered about 5 minutes or until warmed through, stirring several times. Cover pot with lid.

Hang the Dutch oven on a tripod, 8" to 10" above the heat. Let simmer 30 to 45 minutes, uncovering to stir every 15 minutes. Move the pot higher or lower to adjust the heat. Let rest 5 to 10 minutes to thicken before serving. *(If you don't want to use a tripod, set the Dutch oven directly on a ring of hot coals with a few more on the lid. Use just enough heat to maintain a simmer.)*

Try Trappey's jalapeño navy beans with slab bacon in place of plain navies. Yee-ha!

HOMEMADE CORNBREAD

You'll Need

½ C. flour

½ C. sugar

2 tsp. salt

½ tsp. baking soda

1½ C. yellow cornmeal

1 C. buttermilk

2 eggs, beaten

1 C. milk

2 T. butter, melted

Directions

Grease a **10" Dutch oven**. In a large bowl, mix the flour, sugar, salt, baking soda, and cornmeal. Add the buttermilk and mix well. Whisk in eggs, milk, and butter until well blended. Pour batter into the pot and cover with lid.

Set the Dutch oven on a ring of 7 hot coals and place about 15 coals on the lid. Bake 35 to 45 minutes or until a toothpick inserted in the center comes out clean. Rotate the pot and lid several times during cooking and replenish coals as needed to maintain heat. Near the end of cooking time, move a few coals toward the center of lid to increase browning.

This sweet cornbread can be stack-cooked with the chili (page 52) or other simmering dishes. Just set the 10" Dutch oven filled with cornbread batter on top of the partially cooked 12" oven filled with chili. The heat from the 12" lid becomes the bottom cooking ring for the cornbread.

HAM & TATERS

serves 8

You'll Need

- 5 or 6 medium potatoes, washed well
- 1 C. diced ham
- ⅓ C. chopped onion
- ⅓ C. diced red or green bell pepper
- 1 to 2 (10.7 oz.) cans cream of mushroom soup
- ¼ tsp. onion powder
- ½ tsp. garlic powder
- ¼ tsp. salt
- ¼ tsp. black pepper
- ¼ C. grated Parmesan cheese

Directions

Grease a **10" Dutch oven**. Thinly slice the potatoes into a bowl; rinse and drain well. Add the ham, onion, bell pepper, soup, onion powder, garlic powder, salt, and pepper; stir to combine. Spread potato mixture in the pot and cover with lid.

Set the Dutch oven on a ring of 9 hot coals and place about 13 coals on the lid. Cook 35 to 40 minutes or until potatoes are tender. Rotate pot and lid several times during cooking and allow coals to burn down. Remove the lid and sprinkle with cheese; cover and cook 5 to 10 minutes more.

Make this dish as saucy as you like with the amount of soup you use. For a cheesier version, sprinkle with shredded Cheddar or Colby-Jack cheese near the end of cooking.

This sweet and sassy monkey bread tastes good for breakfast or alongside any meal.

CRAN-ORANGE BREAD

serves 10

You'll Need

- ¾ C. sugar
- 1 (3 oz.) box vanilla cook-and-serve pudding mix (*not instant*)
- Zest and juice from 1 orange
- 2 (12 oz.) tubes refrigerated Texas-style biscuits

- ½ C. butter, melted
- ½ C. dried sweetened cranberries, divided
- 1 C. vanilla ready-to-use frosting

Directions

Grease a **10" Dutch oven** and line it with parchment paper, if desired.

In a bowl, combine the sugar, pudding mix, and orange zest. Cut each biscuit into 4 pieces; dip in melted butter and roll in sugar mixture. Place half the biscuits in the pot and sprinkle with half the cranberries. Top with remaining biscuits and cranberries. Pour any leftover butter and sugar over the top. Cover pot with lid.

Set the Dutch oven on a ring of 9 hot coals and place about 14 coals on the lid. Bake 15 to 25 minutes or until lightly browned, rotating pot and lid once. Near the end of baking time, move a few coals to the center of lid to increase browning on top. Let cool 1 minute and then invert onto a buttered platter, or glaze promptly and serve from pot.

Glaze: Mix frosting with enough orange juice to make a thin glaze. Drizzle over warm biscuits.

Melting butter at the campsite is easy. Just place it in a metal bowl and set it over a few hot coals until it turns to liquid gold.

FIRESIDE LASAGNA

serves 10

You'll Need

1½ lbs. lean ground beef

½ C. diced onion

1 (24 oz.) jar spaghetti sauce

3 eggs

2 C. shredded mozzarella cheese, divided

¼ C. grated Parmesan cheese

2 C. cottage cheese

1½ tsp. dried oregano

1 tsp. garlic powder

14 uncooked lasagna noodles

¾ C. hot water

Directions

Spread about 24 hot coals in a flat layer under a **12" Dutch oven**. Cook beef and onion until meat is crumbly and onion is tender. Transfer to a bowl and stir in sauce. In another bowl, mix eggs, 1¾ cups mozzarella cheese, Parmesan and cottage cheeses, oregano, and garlic powder.

Break 5 noodles to cover bottom of pot. Top with the following layers: ⅓ of the meat mixture, half the cheese mixture, 5 noodles, half the remaining meat mixture, all remaining cheese mixture, last 4 noodles, and rest of meat. Pour hot water around inside edge of pot and cover with lid.

Rearrange 12 of the hot coals in a ring under the Dutch oven and place the rest on lid. Cook 45 minutes or until noodles are tender, rotating pot and lid several times and replenishing coals to maintain temperature. Remove from heat and let rest uncovered for 10 minutes. Before serving, sprinkle with remaining ¼ cup mozzarella and let melt.

BLUEBERRY COBBLER

easy fix

serves 10

You'll Need

- 1 (21 oz.) can blueberry pie filling
- 2 C. fresh or frozen blueberries, thawed and drained
- 1 (15.25 to 18.25 oz.) pkg. yellow or white cake mix
- 1 (12 oz.) can lemon-lime soda
- 2 to 3 T. butter
- Sugar

Directions

Line a **12" Dutch oven** with foil. Spread the pie filling and blueberries evenly in the lined pot.

In a bowl, stir together cake mix and soda until well blended. Spread cake batter evenly over fruit. Dot with butter and sprinkle with sugar. Cover pot with lid.

Set the Dutch oven on a ring of 9 hot coals and place about 15 coals on the lid. Bake 30 to 40 minutes or until cake tests done with a toothpick. Rotate pot and lid several times during baking and replenish coals as needed to maintain cooking temperature. Let cool slightly before serving.

Use your favorite pie fillings and fruit to make many different cobblers. Try sprinkling the top with granola, sliced almonds, or brown sugar before baking. Serve warm or cold with whipped cream or ice cream. Yum!

BREAKFAST PIZZA

serves 6–8

You'll Need

6 brown-and-serve sausage links, sliced

½ C. diced red onion

1 (6.5 oz.) pkg. pizza dough crust mix (plus water as directed)

½ C. diced Canadian bacon

½ C. diced ham

¾ C. diced yellow bell pepper

1½ C. frozen shredded hash browns, partially thawed

1½ C. shredded Italian 5-cheese blend

3 eggs

3 T. milk

Garlic powder and black pepper to taste

Parmesan cheese

Directions

Spread about 25 hot coals in a flat layer under a **12" Dutch oven**. Cook the sausage and onion until meat is brown and onion is tender. Remove from heat and transfer meat mixture to a bowl.

Let pot cool and then wipe out excess grease. Line the pot with foil and grease lightly. Prepare pizza dough with water following package directions. Press dough over the bottom and at least ½" up the sides of pot to form a rim. Sprinkle the sausage mixture, Canadian bacon, ham, bell pepper, hash browns, and cheese blend over crust.

In a bowl, whisk together eggs, milk, garlic powder, and pepper; pour evenly over the ingredients inside the crust. Sprinkle with Parmesan cheese and cover pot with lid.

Set the Dutch oven on a ring of 8 hot coals and place about 17 coals on the lid. Bake 20 to 30 minutes or until crust is golden brown on the bottom and eggs are set. Rotate pot and lid twice during cooking. Move several coals from the bottom to the center of lid during the last 5 minutes to increase browning on top. Lift foil to remove pizza from pot; slice and serve.

CHEESY BACON BREAD

extra
prep time

serves 10

You'll Need

- 12 frozen unbaked dinner rolls, thawed but still cold
- 3 T. butter, melted
- 6 bacon strips, cooked and crumbled
- 1 C. shredded Cheddar, Swiss, or Colby-Jack cheese

Directions

Line a **10" Dutch oven** with foil. Cut each dinner roll into 3 pieces and coat in melted butter. Arrange pieces evenly in pot. Sprinkle bacon and cheese over the top. Cover pot with lid and let dough rise until double in size, about 2 hours.

To bake, set the Dutch oven on a ring of 8 hot coals and arrange about 16 coals on the lid. Bake 25 to 35 minutes or until golden brown on top and bottom and no longer doughy in the center. Rotate pot and lid twice during baking and rearrange coals as needed to maintain cooking temperature and promote browning on top.

Purchase precooked bacon or prep it at home before you go camping. If you've got two Dutch ovens, try stacked cooking when it's time to bake these delicious bread bites.

CHICKEN & RICE

easy meal

serves 4–6

You'll Need

- 1 C. uncooked long-grain white rice
- 1 chicken, cut up
- 1 (1 oz.) packet dry onion soup mix
- 1 (14.5 oz.) can chicken broth
- 1 (10.7 oz.) can cream of mushroom or cream of chicken soup
- Water
- Paprika

Directions

Pour the rice into a **12" Dutch oven**. Arrange chicken pieces over rice and sprinkle with soup mix.

In a bowl, whisk together the broth, soup, and 1 soup can of water. Pour mixture over chicken, but do not stir. Sprinkle with paprika and cover pot with lid.

Arrange 12 hot coals in a ring under the Dutch oven and place about 12 coals on the lid. After food begins to simmer, move 4 coals from the bottom to the top. Cook 60 to 70 minutes or until chicken is done and rice is tender. Rotate pot and lid every 15 minutes and let coals burn down before replenishing. Near the end of cooking time, transfer all the coals to the lid to promote browning.

A simple go-to meal that will satisfy even picky eaters. It fits in a 10" Dutch oven, too – just use fewer coals.

VEGETABLE BEEF SOUP

serves 12–14

You'll Need

- 1½ lbs. ground beef
- 2 (14.5 oz.) cans diced tomatoes, with juice
- 5 C. water
- 5 tsp. beef bouillon granules
- 4 medium potatoes, peeled and cubed
- 2 onions, diced (about 2 C.)
- 4 celery ribs, sliced
- 4 carrots, sliced
- 3 C. frozen corn
- 1 C. chopped cabbage
- 1½ tsp. dried basil
- 1½ tsp. dried oregano
- 2 tsp. minced garlic
- 2 tsp. Worcestershire sauce
- Salt and black pepper

Directions

Set a **deep 12" Dutch oven** on a spread of hot coals and brown the beef until crumbly.

Stir in the tomatoes, water, bouillon, potatoes, onions, celery, carrots, corn, cabbage, basil, oregano, garlic, and Worcestershire sauce. Mix well and season with salt and pepper. Heat mixture to a simmer and then cover pot with lid.

Hang the Dutch oven on a tripod, 8" to 10" above the heat. Let simmer about 1 hour or until vegetables are tender, uncovering to stir every 15 minutes. If soup is boiling, raise the Dutch oven further away from the heat or reduce the number of coals underneath. If more heat is needed, move it closer to the coals. *(To cook the soup without a tripod, set the Dutch oven directly on a ring of hot coals with a few more on the lid. Use just enough heat to maintain a simmer.)*

If you don't feel like browning ground beef, use leftover shredded roast instead. It's a delicious way to clean out the cooler before you head home.

BROWNIE CAKE

easy
fix

serves 15–18

You'll Need

1 (3.9 oz.) pkg. chocolate instant pudding mix

1½ C. milk

1 (18.25 oz.) pkg. chocolate cake mix

1½ C. semi-sweet chocolate chips

Directions

Line a **12" Dutch oven** with parchment paper. In a bowl, whisk together pudding mix and milk until thickened. Stir in cake mix until well combined *(batter will be thick)*. Spread batter in lined pot. Sprinkle evenly with chocolate chips and cover pot with lid.

Set the Dutch oven on a ring of 9 hot coals and place about 17 coals on the lid. Bake 30 to 40 minutes or until cake tests done with a toothpick and edges pull away from sides. Rotate pot and lid and check doneness several times during cooking. Let coals burn down before replenishing a few.

If you love chocolate, this easy dessert will make your taste buds swoon. Serve it with freshly churned ice cream or sweet whipped cream for an extra thrill.

BEEF POT ROAST

extra cook time

serves 8

You'll Need

3 carrots

3 potatoes or sweet
   potatoes

½ C. flour

1 tsp. black pepper

1 (4 to 6 lb.) chuck roast

⅓ C. vegetable oil

¾ C. ketchup

2 tsp. minced garlic

1 (10.5 oz.) can French
   onion soup

1 (14.5 oz.) can beef broth

Directions

Peel the carrots and potatoes; cut them into 2" pieces. Mix the flour and pepper on a large plate and coat all sides of roast in the flour mixture.

Spread about 23 hot coals in a flat layer under a **deep 12" Dutch oven**. Heat the oil and add the roast. Cook 4 to 5 minutes on each side until nicely browned; push the roast to one side of pot. Add the ketchup, garlic, carrots, and potatoes; stir and cook about 5 minutes. Move roast back to the center of pot and arrange some vegetables on each side. Add soup and broth; cover pot with lid.

Rearrange 7 of the hot coals in a ring under the Dutch oven and place remaining coals on the lid. Let food simmer slowly for 2½ to 3 hours or until beef is very tender. Maintain a simmer by letting coals burn down before replacing them. Rotate pot and lid every 15 minutes and check periodically; adjust heat as needed to prevent overcooking.

Turn any fresh seasonal vegetables into a favorite campfire dish when you cook them like this.

VEGGIE BAKE

serves 6–8

You'll Need

Water

8 C. bite-size fresh vegetables, any combination (cauliflower or broccoli florets, baby carrots, mushrooms, onions, bell peppers, butternut squash, and/or sweet potatoes)

Garlic powder, salt, and black pepper to taste

¼ C. butter

Grated Parmesan cheese

Directions

Spread about 24 hot coals in a flat layer. Pour ¼" water into a **10" Dutch oven** and set the pot on the hot coals. Add the vegetables and season generously with garlic powder, salt, and pepper. Slice the butter over the top and cover pot with lid.

Cook until steam escapes from lid, 10 to 15 minutes. Remove about half the coals and continue to cook vegetables until fork-tender, 5 to 7 minutes more. Remove Dutch oven from heat. Uncover and tip pot slightly to remove excess water with a baster. Sprinkle with cheese and more pepper before serving.

Prefer roasted vegetables? Toss fresh ones with 2 tablespoons vegetable oil and season well; sauté in a hot pot until partially cooked. Add a drizzle of water, cover pot with lid, and cook with half the coals under Dutch oven and half on top, just until tender. Stir frequently. Top with butter and cheese before serving.

49

PEACH RASPBERRY PIE

serves 8

You'll Need

- ⅔ C. sugar, plus more for sprinkling
- ⅓ C. flour
- ¼ C. brown sugar
- 1 tsp. ground cinnamon
- ½ tsp. ground ginger
- ¼ tsp. ground nutmeg
- ½ tsp. salt
- 4½ C. peeled, sliced peaches *(about 6)*
- 2 T. lemon juice
- 1 T. vanilla
- 1 (14.1 oz.) pkg. refrigerated pie crusts
- 1 C. mashed raspberries
- ¼ C. butter

Directions

Combine ⅔ cup sugar, flour, brown sugar, cinnamon, ginger, nutmeg, salt, peaches, lemon juice, and vanilla; set aside.

Press one crust into a 9" metal pie plate. Pour half the peach mixture into pie shell; spoon raspberries over the top. Spread with remaining peach filling and dot with butter. Place remaining crust over filling and seal crusts together; flute edges as desired. Cut slits in top crust and sprinkle with sugar.

Set pie plate on a riser in a **deep 12" Dutch oven** *(see page 4)*. Cover pot with lid. Set the Dutch oven on a ring of 9 hot coals and place about 17 coals on the lid. Bake 50 to 60 minutes or until golden brown and bubbly. Rotate pot and lid several times and replenish coals as needed. Near the end of cooking time, add several hot coals to the center of lid for browning. Cool completely before slicing.

HEARTY CAMPFIRE CHILI

You'll Need

2 lbs. ground beef

2 lbs. ground turkey

1 onion, diced

2 bell peppers, diced
(red, yellow, orange
and/or green)

1 (45 oz.) jar chunky garden
spaghetti sauce

2 (14.5 oz.) cans diced
tomatoes with juice

1 (15 oz.) can chili beans

1 T. chili powder
(or more to taste)

2 T. dry ranch dressing mix

1 T. dry brown gravy mix,
optional

Salt and black pepper
to taste

Directions

Spread about 18 hot coals in a flat layer under a **12" Dutch oven**. Cook the beef, turkey, and onion until meat is brown and crumbly and onion is tender. Drain off excess grease.

Add bell peppers, spaghetti sauce, tomatoes, beans, chili powder, dressing mix, and gravy mix, if desired. Stir well and season with salt and pepper. Cover pot with lid.

Rearrange about 10 of the hot coals in a ring under the Dutch oven and move remaining coals to the lid. Simmer about 1 hour, rotating pot and lid several times during cooking and uncovering to stir occasionally. Replenish coals as needed to maintain a simmer.

This chili can be simmered on a tripod or used as the base for stacked cooking, too.

Mix up the egg and soup mixtures before leaving home and transport them in airtight containers in your cooler.

BACON EGG BAKE

serves 8–10

You'll Need

- ½ lb. bacon strips, chopped
- ½ lb. ground pork sausage
- 2 C. shredded Cheddar cheese, divided
- 8 bread slices, buttered and cubed
- 10 eggs
- 2¾ C. milk, divided
- 3 T. prepared yellow mustard
- Dash of hot sauce
- 1 (10.7 oz.) can cream of mushroom soup

Directions

Spread about 25 hot coals in a flat layer under a **12″ Dutch oven**. Fry bacon until it just begins to brown. Add sausage and brown both meats until crumbly, stirring often. Remove from heat and drain off excess grease. Reserve ¼ cup cheese for topping; add bread and remaining cheese to meat and stir lightly.

In a bowl, whisk together eggs, 2¼ cups milk, mustard, and hot sauce; pour over bread mixture in pot and let soak 10 minutes. Mix soup with remaining ½ cup milk and pour over the top. Cover pot with lid.

Rearrange 9 of the hot coals in a ring under the Dutch oven and place remaining coals on the lid. Bake 35 to 50 minutes or until eggs are cooked through. Rotate pot and lid every 15 minutes and replenish coals as needed. When done, uncover and sprinkle with reserved cheese; replace lid to let cheese melt.

Try other favorite cheeses and meats, too.

CHICKEN ENCHILADAS

serves 8

You'll Need

1 (28 oz.) can green chile enchilada sauce, divided

15 corn tortillas, divided

3 chicken breast halves, cooked and shredded, divided

Salt and black pepper to taste

1 (10 oz.) pkg. frozen chopped spinach, thawed and squeezed dry, divided

1 (8 oz.) pkg. low-fat cream cheese, divided

1 (4 oz.) can diced green chiles, divided

1¼ C. shredded Mexican cheese blend

Directions

Pour ⅓ of the enchilada sauce into a **10" Dutch oven**. Place a layer of tortillas *(about 5)* over the sauce, tearing them in half and overlapping as needed. Spread half the chicken over tortillas and season with salt and pepper. Spread with half the spinach and half the cream cheese, dropping it by small spoonfuls and spreading lightly. Top with half the green chiles. Repeat layers.

Top with remaining tortillas and sauce, then sprinkle shredded cheese over everything. Cover pot with lid.

Set the Dutch oven on a ring of 8 hot coals and arrange about 14 coals on the lid. Cook 30 to 40 minutes or until cheese is melted and everything is heated through. Rotate pot and lid several times during cooking and move some coals to the center of lid near the end of cooking time. Let rest at least 10 minutes to set up before serving.

SPICY CHILI MAC

serves 5

You'll Need

- 1 lb. ground beef
- 1 onion, chopped
- 2 (10 oz.) cans mild diced tomatoes with green chilies
- 1 C. water
- 1½ C. uncooked rotini pasta or elbow macaroni
- Seasoned salt and black pepper to taste
- ½ C. shredded Cheddar cheese

Directions

Spread about 20 hot coals in a flat layer under a **10" Dutch oven**. Cook the beef and onion until meat is brown and crumbly and onion is tender. Stir in tomatoes with chilies, water, and pasta; sprinkle with seasoned salt and pepper as desired. Bring mixture to a boil and cover pot with lid.

Rearrange 7 of the hot coals in a ring under the Dutch oven and move remaining coals to the lid. Let simmer about 20 minutes or until pasta is tender. Stir after 15 minutes and then rotate pot and lid to finish cooking. Dish it up hot and sprinkle with cheese.

When you begin to smell the food inside your Dutch oven, it's a sign the dish is almost ready to eat!

Serve fresh fruit on the side for a satisfying breakfast, lunch, or dinner.

FRENCH TOAST BAKE

serves 6–8

You'll Need

1 lg. loaf French bread

8 eggs

3 C. milk

¼ C. sugar

1½ tsp. ground cinnamon

½ tsp. salt

2 tsp. vanilla

¼ C. butter

Syrup

Directions

Grease a **12" Dutch oven**. Tear bread into 1" to 2" chunks and toss them into the pot.

In a large bowl, whisk together eggs, milk, sugar, cinnamon, salt, and vanilla until smooth. Pour mixture over the bread and stir lightly. Cut butter into small pieces and scatter over the top. Cover pot with lid

Set the Dutch oven on a ring of 9 hot coals and place about 15 coals on the lid. Bake 45 to 55 minutes or until set and golden brown around edges. Rotate pot and lid several times during baking and replenish coals as needed to maintain cooking temperature. Serve with warm syrup.

Try using eggnog in place of the milk and seasonings for an extra-simple, quick-fix breakfast – yum!

ONE-POT S'MORES BARS

You'll Need

- 1 C. butter, softened
- 1 C. sugar
- 2 eggs
- 2 tsp. vanilla
- 1½ C. flour
- ½ tsp. salt
- 2 tsp. baking powder
- 1½ C. graham cracker crumbs
- 1 (9.3 oz.) pkg. milk chocolate candy bars (6 ct.)
- 2 (7 oz.) jars marshmallow creme

Directions

Line a **12" Dutch oven** with parchment paper. In a large bowl, whisk together butter, sugar, and eggs until light and creamy. Stir in vanilla. Add flour, salt, baking powder, and crumbs; stir well. Spread ⅔ of dough mixture over the bottom of lined pot. Arrange candy bars over dough and cover with spoonfuls of marshmallow creme. Spoon remaining dough over marshmallow layer and cover pot with lid.

Set the Dutch oven on a ring of 8 hot coals and place about 16 coals on the lid. Bake 25 to 35 minutes or until golden brown and cooked through. Rotate pot and lid every 10 minutes, checking frequently and adjusting coals as needed to avoid over-browning on the bottom. Let coals burn down without replenishing.

When marshmallows start to brown, remove 4 coals from the lid and move several of the remaining coals toward the center of lid to finish browning.

INDEX